1st edition, 1st print
Published by Mondå Forlag AS
ISBN: 978-82-93622-15-4

If you have any inquiries, compliments or feedback, please contact us by email at:
info@monda.no

Illustrations: Elise H. Kollerud & Julien S. Bourrelle
Design and layout: Mondå Forlag
Photo credits: Mona Hauglid and Jon Danielsen
Font: Sketchnote Square, Minion Pro and Ubuntu
Print: Livonia Print SIA

www.thescandinavians.net

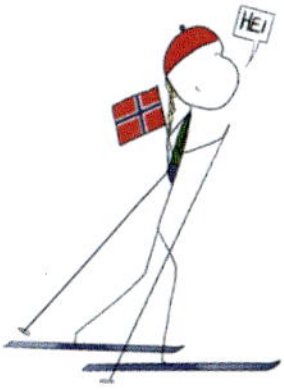
HEI

HEJ!

HEI

Mondå Forlag

The name "Mondå" is inspired by the Spanish word "el mundo", which means "the world". We are a Scandinavian publisher who has been connecting people across cultures since 2013, using humour and simple illustrations.

We help you to see the world from other people's perspectives and to be more conscious about your own culture, perceptions and expectations.

We believe that it is not merely about creating diversity, but about benefitting from diversity.

www.mondabooks.com

Books by Mondå Forlag

Norway

The Social Guidebook to Norway: An illustrated introduction

The Social Guidebook to Norway 2: Friendships and Relationships

The 100 Unwritten Norwegian Social Laws

Norwegian Food: Do they really eat this?

Nordmenn 1 & 2 (in Norwegian)

En smak av norsk kultur (in Norwegian)

The Social Guidebook to Norway (in Chinese)

Sweden

The Swedes: A happy culture of Scandinavia

Working with Swedes

Scandinavia

Cracking the Scandinavian Code

To be published

How Culture Shapes Behaviours

Sånn er nordmenn (in Norwegian)

A word from Elise and Julien

We are pleased that you have chosen to read *Cracking the Scandinavian Code*, and we hope that it will bring you new perspectives and material for reflecting on the Scandinavian culture.This is the first book in the series. It focuses on communication, social behaviours and socialisation.

Julien has been living in Scandinavia for more than 10 years and is originally from Canada, while Elise is Norwegian with Danish heritage. Together, we provide an insider and outsider's view of Scandinavian culture.

Scandinavians will smile and reflect on their own behaviours, social norms and traditions, and how these may be interpreted. Non-Scandinavians will acquire a better understanding of the subtle, unwritten social rules that affect one's ability to communicate effectively with Scandinavians.

This book is a tool to connect people across cultures. We really hope that it will let you see the world from another cultural perspective, and that you will find it useful and entertaining.

You can read more about the story behind our work at the end of the book.

Have fun!

Julien & Elise

www.TheScandinavians.net

The Scandinavians

the.scandinavians

Table of Contents

Preface

How Culture Shapes Behaviours

Scandinavia fascinates the world with the happiness, beauty and wealth of its people. Behind a nearly perfect façade, where the three Scandinavian countries - Denmark, Norway and Sweden - consistently achieve top international rankings, you will find people who may be a little different to what you might have expected. Even Scandinavians themselves do not realise how special and different they are. A lot has to do with their social culture and how they communicate. That is exactly what this book is about.

Scandinavian societies, like every society, have their own traditions, rituals and unwritten social codes. Understanding these codes will tell you a lot about Scandinavians and how they differ from the rest of the world. How to greet others, the distance you should keep during social interactions, the meaning of hand gestures, eye contact, and the different signs of politeness are examples of such social codes. Understanding social codes is the first step to interacting easily with other cultures and to being more aware of our own culture.

Our perception and expectations of other people's behaviours are biased by our own culture. What we perceive or understand from what we hear and see is highly influenced by our cultural background. In other words, the lens through which our brain sees the world shapes our reality. If we can change that lens, not only can we change the way our brain perceives other people's behaviours, but we can allow ourselves to experience the world through completely different perspectives.

This is what “cultural intelligence” is: the ability to understand the impact of individuals’ cultural background on their behaviours. It is essential for effective communication and for socialising with people of different cultures.

When faced with different cultural norms, behaviours and traditions, we either choose to confront, complain or conform. You can refuse to adapt your way of behaving, believing that your way is the right way. You may criticise another society’s beliefs and behaviours. The alternative path is to observe and adapt some of your behaviours to those you live or work with. If you are willing to experience other ways of living and communicating, and refrain from judging norms and values that are different from yours, you will grow and learn more than you could imagine. It is by far the most challenging of the three options, but also the most rewarding.

“Cracking the Scandinavian Code” explains and illustrates some of the most common social behaviours you will encounter in Scandinavia. It is a unique guide to understanding how Scandinavians live and communicate, and to reflecting on culture and cultural differences.

Julien S. Bourrelle

To the tens of thousands of people I spoke for at conferences and corporate events explaining cultural differences these last ten years.

The First Contact

Scandinavians feel more comfortable speaking with others if they have a reason to do so, within the framework of an activity or a group. Spontaneous greetings and attempts to start conversations may be met with scepticism.

If you attempt to start a conversion just because it feels natural to say something - without a clear goal, just to break what you feel is an awkward silence - Scandinavians may start wondering what you are after and be unsure of your intentions.

Come up with a reason when you want to speak with a Scandinavian, and it will feel much more natural to them to answer! Otherwise, Scandinavians may feel you are a little "strange".

Being sceptical of strangers attempting to initiate contact is something that is taught early in a Scandinavian's life. Kids are raised that way.

They are told to be careful around strangers and not to talk to them.

This is in contrast with societies where kids are encouraged to interact with people they do not know; where we teach them to greet, smile and start interactions with strangers, so they can create new relationships.

Greetings

In Southern Europe, like many other places around the world, you try to acknowledge people when entering a room.

In a restaurant, for example, you may nod to the waiter and other guests, who will acknowledge you back. When entering a shop, you will give a greeting, and the cashier will greet you back. Often other customers will turn around and return your greeting with a smile.

In Scandinavia, it works a little bit differently.

Scandinavians refrain from nodding to people, especially if they do not know them. In this way, they make sure that they do not disturb them. Scandinavians are worried about disturbing others. Not disturbing others is good manners in Scandinavia.

While this avoidance of greeting others is part of Scandinavians' "do-not-disturb" politeness, their behaviour may be perceived as cold, uninterested or simply rude abroad. It is all about how one perceives someone else's behaviours and how these behaviours diverge from what is expected.

Do not be surprised if a Scandinavian staying in the hotel room next to yours passes by without looking at or greeting you. As if you did not exist. As if you were invisible. He simply does not want to disturb you! In this way, he is showing respect for your privacy and behaving in a Scandinavian-polite way.

Even Scandinavian neighbours may not greet each other in the hallway if they have not talked to each other before. Scandinavian neighbours need a reason to speak to each other for the first time such as the annual cleaning day at the apartment block where they live. If they do something practical together, then they will need to talk – and then they will greet each other in the hallways!

A similar situation arises at parties and events. In many cultures, people go around and greet everyone personally when they enter a party or an event. They do the same when leaving. It is part of their social norms and an important ritual to follow in order to be perceived as polite.

You go around shaking hands, nodding and sometimes kissing others, including those you haven't met before. It may take half an hour.

Scandinavians will instead try not to disturb others and will, again, tend to greet people they do not know only if there is a practical reason to do so: if they have something specific to discuss with a person, for example.

If you talk with Scandinavians at an event or party, they may leave without coming back to you to say goodbye. Leaving a party without going around to say goodbye to everyone is usually not intended to be rude. They do not want to disturb you by saying goodbye! Maybe you were in the middle of a conversation when they were ready to leave, and they did not want to interrupt!

If Scandinavians do not look at you, greet you or acknowledge your presence, it does not mean they do not like you or that you are not welcome. They just want to give you your space; to leave you alone. Space and being alone are important to Scandinavians.

Scandinavians greet others when there is a practical reason to do so:

- if they have something to discuss,

- if they want to start a conversation,

- or if they need help!

Introduction

In many cultures, when you are talking with a friend and another person you know shows up, you will make sure you introduce your friend to that person. This is considered basic politeness.

In Scandinavia, it works differently. You will be introduced if there is a practical reason for doing so. Otherwise, you may be left standing there, not knowing what to do while your friend is having a quick chat with his friend.

Your Scandinavian friend does not intend to be rude, impolite or display a lack of social education; it is simply more efficient and less risky not to introduce you. It prevents a potentially awkward conversation between people who do not know each other.

Scandinavians want to prevent the awkwardness that can easily happen in an "unframed" communication between people who have not met before, and so they may choose not to introduce you. Yet they may be very keen that you meet their friend another time, and they may mention this as soon as their friend has left!

Scandinavians need a "frame" to speak easily to strangers. This frame is missing when you meet by chance on the street.

Conversations

Scandinavians socialise best when doing something practical rather than simply talking, and you will quickly notice that attempting to ask broad and open questions may lead to somehow uncomfortable situations.

With an acquaintance, Scandinavians will go to a quiz rather than for a coffee. They will play a game rather than discussing the news. They will go walking or bicycling rather than reflecting together on the world.

If you want to discuss politics, sign up to a political organisation. If you want to discuss art, sign up to an art club. If you want to discuss feelings, get an appointment with a psychologist!

Scandinavians' socialisation is more "organised" than what most other cultures are used to.

While in many places around the world, a conversation could look something like this:

Where a simple comment opens the door to an interesting answer, and where the conversation flows easily thereafter.

In Scandinavia, it may not flow as easily and may look more like this:

There is a need for a "frame" around conversations and discussion. This is because unframed discussions are not the usual means of getting to know people.

Without that frame, conversations easily become direct, simple and pragmatic, and often uncomfortable.

Social Logic

In many countries around the world, you may naturally greet strangers and start talking for no reason.

You end up talking for a little while and, maybe, you sit down with the coffee you just ordered and continue the conversation. Doing so, you connect intellectually.

You may then invite each other for a meal, and, after a while, you may decide to organise something together.

That is when you know that you really are starting a new friendship. Let us say that you go berry picking together.

Purposeful activities follow from interesting conversations and a desire to get to know new people, and the typical socialisation timeline looks something like this:

In Scandinavia, things work a little bit differently.

First, you sign up to an organisation or club. Scandinavians have organisations for everything, so you just need to pick one that fits your interest and join their activity. Let us say you sign up for the "blåbärsplockar förening" (Organisation for the Picking of Blueberries).

The first time you join the organisation, you will most probably go straight to the forest and work purposefully for several hours - mostly in silence. Purposeful communication may take place around practical aspects of picking berries.

When you have been part of this organisation for a few months or a few years, doing something practical on a regular basis, you may start to interact outside the secure framework of the organisation. After a while you may end up going for a coffee or a meal with a person you appreciate outside the framework of the organisation.

That is when you know that you really are starting a new friendship.

In Scandinavia, meals are usually not a means of getting to know people. They are a result of an established relationship.

This is key to understanding the Scandinavian socialisation logic. Do not invite a Scandinavian you have just met to share a meal or a coffee. You may never see him again!

Get involved instead. Take part in "frame activities", i.e. organised and purposeful activities. Work voluntarily for an organisation, play a sport, get involved in your neighbourhood or join any type of group.

Frame Activities & Social Bubbles

The more groups you get involved in, the more sociable you will be in Scandinavia. Yet people you get to know through each of these groups will almost never mix with people from the other groups you are part of. Each "frame activity" you take part in will create what I called a "social bubble".

These social bubbles are rigid, and they do not mix! Scandinavians are social within many social bubbles, but people from different bubbles do not interact.

You need to take part in the organised activity in order to be included in the social bubble related to that activity. Outsiders will not be invited to join activities organised within a bubble, even if the activity does not relate to the bubble's "frame activity", and even if the outsiders know several people who are part of the social bubble.

For example, imagine a sports group going to have a beer. It would be challenging to invite someone who is not part of the team to join for the beer, even if that person knows a team player very well.

In many cultures, when you meet someone new that you appreciate, you will try to include that new person within your social network. In Scandinavia, you need to sign up for activities and groups yourself to be included in the associated social networks. Even if you get to know a few Scandinavians well, they will not easily be able to invite you to join their social networks, because you are not part of the activities those social networks are based upon.

The Exit Door

There are many examples of frame activities. Norwegians hiking in the mountains is one such example. Norwegians will readily speak to strangers in the mountains. This is because they are doing the same activity, and that provides a secure framework for socialising. In the mountains or the woods, Scandinavians can also easily escape whenever they want to by walking in the other direction.

Scandinavians need two things to feel comfortable communicating with others:

(1) A frame activity providing a reason to communicate

(2) An opportunity to escape

To connect with Scandinavians, do an activity, a sport or something practical, and always leave them an opportunity to escape. They will feel safe, they will greet you, and they will make small talk for no reason.

The opposite of this is one of the most awkward places I have experienced: a Scandinavian elevator.

You feel a heavy atmosphere. Do not greet anyone, do not talk, do not look at other people, do not smile - it will just make things worse!

In an elevator, you are missing both the frame and the opportunity to escape. This makes it a very uncomfortable place for Scandinavians.

Gifts & Owing

Many cultures around the world build friendships based on a form of giving and receiving. You invite someone for a coffee, for food or give a physical gift to show your interest in that person. If the person is interested in getting to know you, he or she will give back in another way, by inviting you to something, for example.

In such cultures, we build relationships and trust by giving to others and owing to others.

This is uncomfortable for Scandinavians. Scandinavians want things to be equal and are uncomfortable when they owe anything to others. This is especially the case when owing to people they do not know very well.

They will pay for themselves in coffee shops, restaurants and bars, bring their own alcohol to parties and their own food when having lunch together in the forest or in a park. This, despite having known their friends for many years.

They do not do this because they are cold people, but because their understanding of relationships is based on different premises. One premise is that you should not owe anything to others, something that makes it easier to leave relationships, to feel independent. That is another example of the way Scandinavians make sure there is always the opportunity to escape.

In business, the same thing happens. Inviting potential clients for lunch, for example, can quickly become problematic. This is because gifting anything to someone in business is seen as a form of corruption! Sporting events tickets, dinners, lunch or even a coffee can quickly be frowned upon and seen as an attempt to "buy a favour".

If you plan to do business with Scandinavians, be wary of paying for a lunch before the collaboration is confirmed and signed. Sometimes it is even better not to do so before the collaboration is over and it is time to celebrate together.

If you force Scandinavians to accept you paying for something, they may suddenly avoid you. The project you were discussing will not be realised because you have put them in a situation where they have received something from you, and where collaborating with you could be seen as payback.

The same logic applies when having a drink with acquaintances. Scandinavians will most probably feel uncomfortable if you pay for their beer. They will feel they owe you something and will keep thinking about it. If they do not want another beer, they may ask how much they owe you for the beer you paid for.

They want to be polite and re-establish an equilibrium where no one owes anything to others. This is how Scandinavians feel most comfortable. Learn to connect with Scandinavians in the independent way they are used to, and everything will be just fine.

If you are invited to a barbecue or a dinner at someone's home, do not be surprised if your host sends a message afterwards and asks you to share in the cost of the food. You are also often expected to bring your own alcohol to dinners or evenings with friends.

Food

Food and drink have different meanings in Scandinavia, and between Scandinavian countries.

While high quality and refined food presented in a delicate way is a sign of appreciation and welcome in many cultures, in Norway food is seen more as something you eat in order to survive. Even by Scandinavian standards, Norwegians lunches are something of their own.

Swedes and Danes are more refined in their culinary traditions and will eat varied warm lunches.

Emotions

The way Scandinavians express feelings is subtle. Refrain from showing negative feelings - anger, frustration or any type of aggression. You may express positive feelings, but keep it subtle.

Be excited without moving your body. Be happy in silence - except when watching football or cross-country skiing, or when drinking!

Unless you come from Finland, Scandinavian emotional feedback will be challenging to interpret.

Elise and I were invited to the wedding of a friend. He was from Lebanon and she was Scandinavian. From the very beginning of the wedding, it was easy to identify the two families. Emotions were expressed quite differently.

Luckily, during the dinner, the Lebanese started to play music while the Danes, Norwegians and Swedes started to drink.

After an hour, the Scandinavians were dancing on the tables, and both families connected very well!

Alcohol helps Scandinavians to express emotions and to be sociable, and the contrast can be shocking! I like to say that Scandinavians are much easier to interact with when they have been drinking a little. Sometimes you do not even need to wait until they have started to drink – you can often observe a change in their emotions and social abilities when they just have a beer in their hands!

There are differences between the Scandinavian countries here. In Denmark, for example, you can have a beer at lunch, or drink a beer while you are working as a barman. If you do that in Norway, you may be seen as an alcoholic by your colleagues, or risk losing your job!

Eye Contact

Scandinavians will look each other in the eye a lot when talking with colleagues at work or with friends. Looking others in the eye when talking to them is a mark of respect in Scandinavia and is expected, even when you disagree.

Cultures around the world have different eye-contact rituals. In certain cultures, you will avoid eye contact with people in positions of authority - your boss for example - or people of higher social status. You also do this as a mark of respect.

In Scandinavia, everyone is more or less equal, and you should maintain eye contact in discussions. If you look down or away, Scandinavians might think that you are uninterested, that you do not care, or that you are annoyed.

While they do maintain eye contact in discussions, most foreigners will experience Scandinavians as people who avoid eye contact! This is because they avoid looking at others unless they have a reason to – just as they avoid greeting others without a reason.

They will avoid eye contact with strangers when entering a place for example, and only attempt eye contact with people they know if they want to start a conversation.

Social norms in many cultures tell us to look at people when entering a restaurant or an event, or when one wants to exit from public transport. This is not common in Scandinavia. Scandinavians will refrain from looking strangers in the eye. They do not want to disturb other people. They will arrive silently at the bus stop, avoid eye contact with the other people standing there, and hope no one has noticed they are there.

Personal Space

This is when you know that a Scandinavian bus stop is full, and that you need to stand.

This is not something new, and it has nothing to do with the pandemic or the government imposing rules on social distancing. It has always been like this. Scandinavians really love their personal space, and they will be sure to leave space when standing near others as well. Keeping one to two metres apart from strangers was already part of the Scandinavian social culture, decades before the pandemic.

The social rules applied by governments around the world to limit the spread of coronavirus are scarily similar to the normal way Scandinavians interacted before the pandemic.

Take conferences and parties, for example, where a foreigner might start to talk to a Scandinavian. The foreigner would speak at a distance that felt comfortable to him. The Scandinavian, feeling his personal space invaded, would take a small step back.

The foreigner, being interested to get to know the Scandinavian, would step closer, thus re-establishing what he felt to be a comfortable distance.

That distance would not be comfortable for the Scandinavian, who would step back again - and so a little dance would begin!

The social rules requiring everyone to stand one to two metres apart make the world a much more comfortable place for Scandinavians.

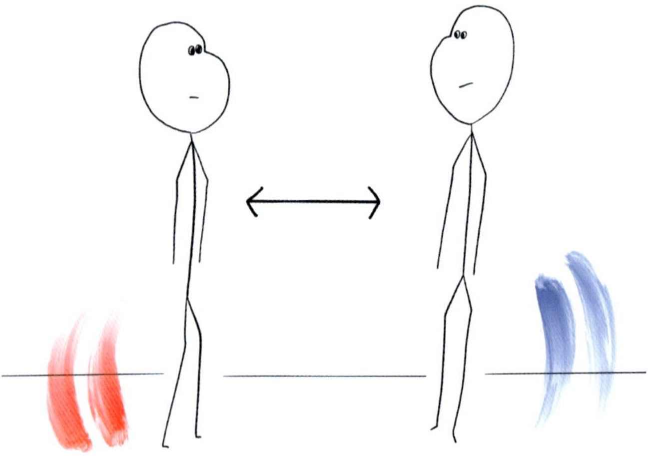

When the world goes back to normal and we can travel again, Scandinavians will still need a lot of space, making it easy to spot them again when they are abroad.

This need for space is linked to the Scandinavian desire not to disturb others.

Last time Elise and I were in Thailand, we observed two Danes speaking to each other, both sitting alone at two different tables. They each sat alone at their own table in order to make sure the other could leave whenever he wanted!

It will take many days for these new acquaintances to take the very uncomfortable step of asking to sit together. Until then, they prefer to sit at their own tables and speak to each other from there. Doing so leaves an easier "exit door" and makes communication less awkward.

Being Alone

Scandinavians value their personal space as much as their opportunities to be alone.

They will travel alone to work, rather than arranging to commute with colleagues. It is much more efficient and practical, and you do not need to talk to anyone.

In addition to the need for space, this explains why Scandinavian buses looked like this a long time before the pandemic.

This is when you know that a bus is full and that you need to stand!

At weekends and on public holidays, Scandinavians will leave as soon as possible to go to their hytter, sommarstugor or sommerhus. Many Scandinavians like to spend their money on being alone and living simply, close to nature.

Norwegians are the most extreme here. They will spend a large part of their savings to buy such a place to be alone in the middle of nowhere. They will leave work early on Fridays to go there. Do not plan any meetings after 11.30! Some Norwegians even have one cabin in the mountains and one by the ocean.

In Nature

Norway has fantastic fjords and mountains, Sweden has lakes, hills and forests, and Denmark is flat, windy and sandy. There is no nature in Denmark for Swedes and Norwegians, but Danes have beaches.

Danes are more continental; they enjoy their summer houses by the sea with a good beer. Swedes have beautiful wooden houses by the lakes, which they also like to visit on warmer days. Norwegians have small houses in the mountains, which they call "hytter" and visit all year long. From these "hytter" they climb mountains, often alone.

Do not be surprised to see Norwegians in the mountains when it is raining, snowing or windy, with no other goal than to reach the top of the mountain and come back to their "hytte". Norwegians are even called "mountain monkeys" by other Scandinavians!

Scandinavians will proudly go outdoors in difficult weather conditions. They do not talk: the wind and rain make it impossible. It gives them a great feeling, a feeling of accomplishment.

"There is no such thing as bad weather, only bad clothing."

Kids are forced to go outside in harsh conditions from a young age. When they have done it enough times, they also start to believe that this is enjoyable. This is exactly how culture transmits itself from generation to generation.

Danes bicycle so often in the rain that it just becomes normal and part of their routine. To suffer becomes part of their daily routine, their social norms, and they soon forget that there are other ways to commute.

Need to Suffer & Scandinavian Safety

Scandinavians enjoy physical pain - or at least, to some of us outsiders, it seems like they do.

Pain does not really exist for Scandinavians. It is not sufferance, it is enjoyment.

Jumping into cold fjords and lakes, rolling in the snow naked, jogging on icy roads in the winter darkness, or bicycling in freezing rain and wind every day.

By having some level of physical pain, everything else seems more comfortable to Scandinavians: their apartments in the dark days of the year, their cabins, their offices, etc.

Scandinavians make sure they teach their kids from a very young age to enjoy suffering.

Leaving babies outside in sub-zero temperatures is not only a way to introduce them to the need to suffer, it is also a sign that society is still safe, and that you can take a coffee inside a coffee shop and not worry about your baby sleeping in its pram outside on the pavement.

Sports

This is a great way to connect with Scandinavians. Not only is it a "frame activity", but you also suffer together without talking too much. This is the best way to bond with Scandinavians.

Cross-country skiing, or Nordic skiing, is a sport often practised alone in the dark in freezing temperatures.

It requires no communication.

It is a very Scandinavian sport, practised mostly by Swedes and Norwegians.

"Birkebeinerrennet" (Birken) is a 54 km ski race over mountains and valleys in Norway. Vasaloppet is a similar race in Sweden. Swedes take it to an even higher level; there you need to ski over 90km!

Thousands of Scandinavians participate, including representatives from the business sector and the royals.

While Danes tend not to be as interested in Nordic skiing as Swedes and Norwegians, as there is little snow in Denmark, the Danish Crown Prince still took part in both Birken and Vasaloppet.

By showing publicly that you have great physical abilities, that you are in good shape and that you endure pain in the cold for several hours in silence, you will increase your credibility, trust and respect.

These races are also an expression of how safe Scandinavian societies still are. Where else in the world would it be safe for future kings to ski in public for several hours?

Or to see the Crown Princess bicycling to pick up her kids at kindergarten?

It is important for the royals in Scandinavia to live close to the people. This is part of their role. People bicycle to work and to kindergarten, and so the royals should try to show that they do the same.

Scandinavian Comfort

While Scandinavians enjoy suffering, they also enjoy comfort in ways that may be surprising to outsiders.

A Swedish woman may show up for a formal event in a dress and running shoes. Running shoes are more comfortable and better for her back than elegant high heels. It is more important to be comfortable than formal.

A Norwegian businessman may wear a full suit and carry his laptop in a backpack, so he is comfortable using both his hands.

While it may be seen around the world as a lack of politeness or education not to wear appropriate clothing, shoes or accessories, for Scandinavians, it is just more practical and comfortable.

Danes are again a little more continental here. They tend to dress more formally at work, and to relax more during evening events. This contrasts with Norwegians, who tend to dress informally during the day, but like to wear more formal clothing for evening gatherings. This can lead to funny situations when they meet for dinner.

Politeness

In Scandinavia, politeness is mostly about not disturbing others. Respecting privacy, space and silence is often more important than following internationally recognised norms of politeness.

Social codes, norms and manners are different in Scandinavia and may be surprising to outsiders.

You do not disturb someone by greeting them without a specific purpose. You avoid speaking loudly in public places to respect others' right to calm. You avoid looking at someone for no reason. You leave space, both physically and psychologically.

Scandinavians are practical, purposeful and efficient in their politeness, and since Scandinavians are polite and want to prevent confrontation, they won't tell you if you are being impolite in their eyes.

When they write emails, Scandinavians have a tendency to get straight to the point, and they use few of the expressions of politeness people in most countries are used to. They will also use pretty much the same type of language if they write to a secretary or to a top executive.

The direct and pragmatic way Scandinavians communicate by email may easily be misinterpreted. If a Scandinavian is direct in his or her communication, and lacks all forms of written politeness, it usually does not mean that he or she is annoyed or angry. It is just a highly transactional and efficient way to communicate and to get things done.

Nice to see you again

[redacted]

To: "Julien S. Bourrelle" <julien@monda.no>

Hei, se vedlegg. Mvh Sverre

On Sun, [redacted] at 2:47 PM Julien S. Bourrelle <julien@monda.no> wrote:

> Hi Sverre,
>
> it was a pleasure to meet you today. I enjoyed our conversation very much!
>
> You mentioned a report that I should read. I would love it if you could send it to me.
>
> Have a lovely day,
>
> Best regards,
>
> Julien

Wild Cats, Coconuts and Peaches

A great way to summarise this book is to think of a wild cat.

In order to tame a wild cat, you need to be slow, careful, playful and distant. You need to play games for hours, days or years.

It is a little bit the same when meeting and getting to know Scandinavians.

They may feel hard from the outside. Just like a coconut, hard on the outside, but very nice inside.

Give it a little bit of time.

Give them space.

Be independent.

Invite them with care.

Control your emotions.

Involve yourself.

Enjoy Scandinavians!

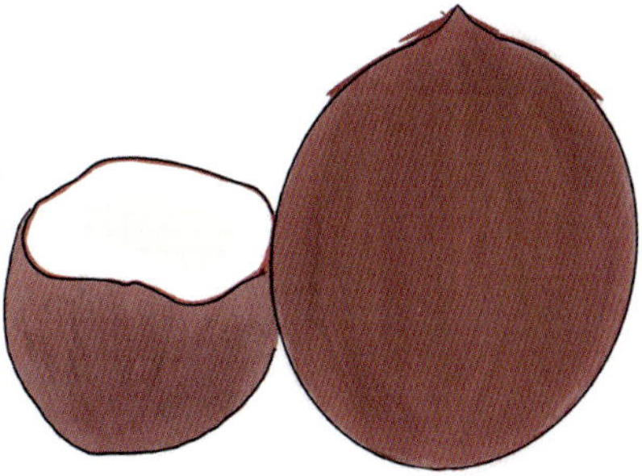

Julien S. Bourrelle

MSc. Rocket Science

Made in Canada

Lived in Australia, Canada, Germany, New Zealand, Spain, Norway

Speaks French, English, Spanish, Norwegian

Email: julien@monda.no

Instagram: @juliensbourrelle

Facebook: Julien S. Bourrelle

Elise H. Kollerud

BSc. Nursing & Sociology

75% Norwegian, 25% Danish

Publisher & Illustrator at Mondå Forlag

Email: elise@monda.no

Instagram: @forlagssjefen

From Canada to Scandinavia

As Steve Jobs said: "You can never connect the dots looking forward, you can only connect the dots looking backwards". At twenty years old, Julien could only speak French and had never been outside Canada. Ten years later, he could speak four languages fluently and had lived in five countries.

Julien studied mechanical engineering at McGill University in Montréal, with stays at the University of Western Australia and at the University of Auckland. He specialised in astrodynamics, a sub-field of rocket science at the Technical University of Munich and the Polytechnic University of Madrid under a scholarship from the European Commission. After finishing his master's degree, he moved to a little town in the middle of Norway by the name of Trondheim to take a doctoral degree at the Norwegian University of Science and Technology (NTNU).

Each time Julien moved to a different country, he made a conscious effort to adapt his behaviours to the local norms, to learn the language and to integrate within the society. His adaptation to Norway and Scandinavia has been the most challenging cultural experience of his life and the starting point of this cultural project.

When he finally cracked the Scandinavian code, he started to help others understand these peculiar Nordic people. He became the first foreigner to sit on the board of directors of the Norwegian University of Science and Technology since the foundation of the university in 1910, he led the doctoral organisation and he sat on the Norwegian National Research committee (UHR). He took leave from his doctoral studies to start lecturing on the Norwegian culture in 2013 and founded the publishing house Mondå Forlag.

In 2015, he received the Top 10 award from HRH Crown Prince Haakon which highlights an "outstanding international role model in the Norwegian working and social life".

This award provided him with great motivation to continue developing tools that bridge cultures.

Elise took over the leadership of Mondå Forlag, and together they expanded to Sweden in 2016 with the publication of their first book there. Julien started to lecture about Swedish and Scandinavian culture the year after, using the simple cultural illustrations drawn by Elise. Mondå Forlag went on to publish books from several authors in the years that followed.

In 2018, Julien started to lecture internationally on Scandinavian culture and global cultural differences. He gave two TEDx lectures and spoke for hundreds of large companies and organisations, including NATO, Statoil, Geberit, the Central Bank of Norway, booking.com, PWC and embassies.

Elise and Julien work as a team, both in their private lives and within the Mondå project. They are both involved in the writing, designing and illustrating of their work. Elise and Julien travel together to Julien's lectures and host events together on stage.

You can read more about Julien's keynote lectures and courses on **www.juliensbourrelle.com**

"We all would benefit better from diversity if locals and foreigners were provided with adequate tools to understand each other's biases, expectations and perceptions."

THANK YOU:

Sebrina Puggaard

Pierre Wilhelm Puggaard

Astrid Rose Hegnar

Claire Cooper

Marius Monsås Svenungsen

Helene Halvorsen Kollerud

Kristian Øye Birgirsson

Online cultural resources

www.thescandinavians.net

www.fb.com/thescandinavians

Country specific

www.theswedes.net (Sweden)

www.thesocialguidebook.no (Norway)

Lectures and Courses

www.juliensbourrelle.com